AT THE Aquarium

WONDERFUL WHALES

by
Mignonne Gunasekara

BEARPORT PUBLISHING

Minneapolis, Minnesota

PHOTO CREDITS

All images are courtesy of Shutterstock.com, unless otherwise specified. With thanks to Getty Images, Thinkstock Photo and iStockphoto. Plant Vectors Throughout – Baksiabat, MicroOne. Front Cover & Recurring Images – Sanjatosic, Miles Away Photography, MicroOne, Baksiabat, Craig Lambert Photography, wildestanimal. 2–3 – Orla. 4–5 – sergemi, Pod_Monodon_ monoceros, CampCrazy Photography, Joanne Weston, Nico Faramaz, Tomas Kotouc, wildestanimal, Rich Carey, Martin Prochazkacz. 6–7 – PHOTO JUNCTION, Jitinatt Jufask, aDam Wildlife. 8–9 – Deep OV, wildestanimal. 10–11 – Paul S. Wolf, rangizzz, Tomas Kotouc. 12–13 – Macgork, wildestanimal. 14–15 – Allexxandar, Andrew Sutton, Chase Dekker, K_Dreamcatcher. 16–17 – Damsea, Graeme Snow, Joanne Weston. 18–19 – CampCrazy Photography, Luna Vandoorn3, MK photograp55. 20–21 – Dr. Kristin Laidre, Irina Markova, VBakunin68. 22–23 – David Pereiras, DejaVuDesigns, Rich Carey. 24 – Public_P, Rich Carey.

Library of Congress Cataloging-in-Publication Data is available at www.loc.gov or upon request from the publisher.

ISBN: 978-1-64747-408-9 (hardcover)
ISBN: 978-1-64747-415-7 (paperback)
ISBN: 978-1-64747-422-5 (ebook)

For more information, write to Bearport Publishing, 5357 Penn Avenue South, Minneapolis, MN 55419.
Printed in the United States of America.

CONTENTS

WELCOME TO THE AQUARIUM!

Welcome to the aquarium! Aquariums look after sea animals. Many aquariums do lots of work to protect wild animals, too.

Today, we will be looking at whales. Whales are mammals. This means they are warm-blooded animals that feed their babies milk from their bodies.

Warm-blooded animals can keep their bodies warm whether it's hot or cold outside.

BRYDE'S WHALE

Bryde's whales eat fish and small **crustaceans** called krill.

These whales live in warm waters.

Bryde's whales spend most of their time alone or with one other whale.

Brydeʼs whales are **baleen** whales. Baleen is made of the same stuff as human hair and nails.

A baleen whale uses baleen in its mouth to **filter** food out of the water.

SOUTHERN RIGHT WHALE

Southern right whales usually have white patches on their heads.

This whale's white patches are made up of other small animals.

Southern right whales are baleen whales. They have hundreds of pieces of baleen in their mouths.

These whales can be over 50 feet (15.2 m) long.

Southern right whales are slow swimmers.

HUMPBACK WHALE

Male humpback whales sing.

A humpback whale song can last for hours and travel very far. Many people think the male whale sings to get female whales to notice him.

In the summer, these whales live at the top and bottom of Earth. In winter, they travel to the middle part of Earth.

Humpback whales come together to have young in the winter.

Humpback whales can be found in every ocean on Earth.

SPERM WHALE

Sperm whales dive deep to hunt for fish, sharks, and squid.

Sperm whales live in family groups called **pods.** Mothers in pods take turns looking after babies.

You can spot a sperm whale by its huge head and round forehead. The head makes up about one-third of the whale's whole body!

The sperm whale has the largest brain of any animal.

BLUE WHALE

Blue whales can be found in every ocean on Earth.

Blue whales are baleen whales and mostly eat krill. These whales may be huge, but the krill they eat are tiny.

Blue whales grow to be more than 100 feet (30.5 m) long. That's the size of some planes!

Blue whales usually live for around 90 years in the wild.

The blue whale is the largest animal that has ever lived. It is even bigger than any dinosaur!

MINKE WHALE

There are two kinds of minke whales. They are the smallest of the baleen whales.

Minke whales can live to be 50 years old.

Minke whales live in groups. They make sounds to talk to one another and find food.

BELUGA WHALE

Beluga whales are also known as white whales.

Baby belugas are born a dark color. They turn white as they get older.

Beluga whales can dive deeper than half a mile (900 m). They can hold their breath for over 20 minutes at a time.

Belugas can live for up to 50 years.

NARWHAL

The narwhal is also known as the unicorn of the sea.

A male narwhal can grow a very long, swirly **tusk** that sticks out of its top lip. This tusk is actually a tooth!

Narwhals live in the cold waters of the Arctic Ocean. They need to watch out for polar bears that hunt and eat them.

Narwhals dive deep to hunt for shrimp, fish, and squid.

THANKS FOR VISITING!

Trash in the ocean is a big problem for whales.

Thank you for stopping by the aquarium. If you like wonderful whales, there are things you can do to keep them safe.

It is important to keep trash from getting into the oceans. Pick up any garbage you see lying around and **recycle** what you can.

Why not take part in a beach cleanup with your friends?

GLOSSARY

baleen something found in the mouths of some whales that is used to filter food out of the water

crustaceans animals that live in water and have a hard outer shell

filter to remove wanted materials by passing through something

pods groups of whales or dolphins that live together

recycle to turn something used and unwanted into something new

tusk a long, pointed tooth

INDEX